D0175448

To: _____

From: _____

DWELL

Celebrating the Arrival of

ADVENT *at* HOME

DWELL

Celebrating the Arrival of

ADVENT *at* HOME

DEXTERITY
NASHVILLE

604 Magnolia Lane
Nashville, TN 37211

Copyright © 2020

All rights reserved. Except as permitted by the US Copyright Act of 1976, no part of this book may be reproduced, distributed, or transmitted without prior written permission from the publisher. For information, please contact info@dexteritycollective.co.

Scripture quoted by permission. Quotations designated (NET) are from the NET Bible® copyright ©1996, 2019 by Biblical Studies Press, L.L.C. http://netbible.com. All rights reserved.

New Revised Standard Version Bible, copyright © 1989 the Division of Christian Education of the National Council of the Churches of Christ in the United States of America. Used by permission. All rights reserved.

Printed in the United States of America.

First edition: 2020
10 9 8 7 6 5 4 3 2 1

ISBN: 978-1-947297-21-0 (Hardcover)
ISBN: 978-1-947297-22-7 (eBook)

Library of Congress Cataloging-in-Publication Data

Title: Dwell : celebrating the arrival of Advent at home.
Description: Nashville, TN: Dwell, 2020.
Identifiers: ISBN: ISBN: 978-1-947297-21-0 (Hardcover) | ISBN: 978-1-947297-22-7 (eBook)
Subjects: LCSH Advent. | Advent--Prayers and devotions. | Christmas--Prayers and devotions. | Families--Religious life. | BISAC RELIGION / Christian Living / Devotional
Classification: LCC BX2170.A4 D94 2020 | DDC 242/.332--dc23

Book and cover design by Sarah Siegand.
Editorial development by Krystal Ribble.

DWELL:

To live as a resident

Jesus replied, *"If anyone loves me, he will obey my word, and my Father will love him, and we will come to him and take up RESIDENCE with him."*
John 14:23 NET

Jesus answered him, *"Those who love me will keep my word, and my Father will love them, and we will come to them and make our HOME with them."*
John 14:23 NRSV

Contents

Introduction

As the air grows crisp and the trees drop their leaves, we look forward to the most beloved holiday of the year: Christmas.

For many, the lead up to this holiday is commemorated at home through the observance of Advent. That often means finding one or two ways to count down to December 25th, the day we celebrate Jesus's birth. But there are many ways we can celebrate the coming of the Messiah in every area of our homes.

In this book you will find a flow through FIVE spaces in your home that symbolizes the way many of us emotionally navigate this special holiday. We will journey through your Living Room, Dining Room, Kitchen, Activity Space, and finally your Christmas Space.

In each room:

We first <u>ANTICIPATE</u> the coming of Jesus.

We take joy in the <u>ARRIVAL</u> of Jesus.

We are <u>AWAKENED</u> to who He is.

We then recognize His <u>ANOINTING</u> as the true Savior of the world.

And finally, we praise Him with <u>ADORATION</u> for all He has done and will do for mankind.

DWELL

This book is designed to help you find ways to invite the Lord into your celebration this year, while also sharing God's Word and promises with your family along the way.

We hope this book of reflections becomes a daily source of peace during this busy but sacred time of year, and that it serves to remind you of the true meaning of the season. Each devotional day will offer activities to help you take hold of the scriptures you are reading. They are also great activities to do with your family and friends as you set aside special time to focus on Advent, leading up to Christmas Day.

Please allow this Advent devotional to bring the calming presence of the Lord into your home, and feel free to participate in as many or as few of the activities as make sense for your family this season.

We hope you enjoy this journey through your home as you look at the Christmas story in new and exciting ways this season.

CELEBRATING ADVENT IN THE

Living Room

The world needed a Savior.

Many people longed for a political Savior. Some wanted a religious Savior. The Savior to come would rescue God's people in every way that matters, but He would not look like they had imagined. This Savior could have come in a million different ways, but as a baby born to a poor couple from the unimportant town of Nazareth?

No one could have seen this coming.

There had been hints and promises of a Savior earlier in Scripture, and Moses continued laying the foundation for the arrival of the Messiah in Deuteronomy. While the other nations trusted in mediums and enchanters and fortune-tellers, Moses told the Israelites that they would receive a future Prophet who would come and shake their entire world into clarity:

The Lord your God will raise up for you a prophet like me from among your own people; you shall heed such a prophet.
– Deuteronomy 18:15

Imagine what the people must have thought when they heard that the Great Prophet would be one of their own—a brother who was just like them.

What emotions must have swirled around in their hearts?

Could they have pictured a baby in a manger who would learn to walk and talk and join their children in games? Could they have imagined the rough hands of a carpenter? Could they think of the Messiah as someone so ordinary looking that they could pass Him in the streets each day without a second thought?

This would, in fact, be the man who would save the world from sin.

Jesus may have looked ordinary, but He only looked that way. And while some people may have worried that such an average-looking man could not possibly fulfill all their expectations, Jesus is better than anything they could have imagined.

In your own life, as you approach Advent and the anticipation the season brings for Jesus's arrival, who is it that you need? How is Jesus the answer to the longings of your heart?

Do you need a Prophet for your future? Do you need a Savior for your life? Who is the Lord to you and what traits of His do you celebrate as you lead up to Christmas?

During Advent, we prepare our homes to celebrate the birth of Jesus. In many homes, this begins in the main living space of the home: the Living Room.

One way to look forward to Christmas is by putting something in the living room that can be referenced *every day*, to

count down to the birth of Jesus and remind us of the Savior we desperately need. We can do this with an Advent banner.

Each day, as you use your Advent banner to count down to Jesus's arrival, look at your family members and ponder these thoughts:

Imagine what it must have been like for the Israelite families of Moses's day when they heard that the True Prophet was going to come from among their own people. What a wonderful feeling to know that the Savior would one day live among you!

As you look at your family, know that the Savior is here. He is there in the room with you, right where you are. What a wonderful feeling to know He is here, and what a beautiful season to celebrate His coming into our lives!

Advent Prayer

Lord, thank You for moments to reflect on Jesus's birth and what it means for all mankind. Thank You for Jesus's humanity, that He was able to sympathize with us in our weakness; and thank You for His divinity, that He was born without sin to be the Savior the world so desperately needed.

Advent Activity

Create an Advent banner, or garland, with twenty-five little pockets, one for every day of December leading up to Christmas Day. These types of banners can be purchased at a store, or you can make one out of cloth or paper.

The banner offers a daily reminder to keep the coming of the Savior at the center of life in your home during Advent.

If you do not have a banner already, you can use the following materials to make an easy and personalized countdown calendar for the Advent season.

MATERIALS:

- **Yarn or ribbon** –Measure the space you wish to hang the banner (e.g., a banister, mantle, or wall) to gauge how long the yarn or ribbon should be.
- **Paper or fabric** – Estimate enough for 25 rectangles and 25 triangles. Think of making each rectangle about the size of a one-dollar bill. The triangles should have a bottom edge that is slightly longer than the short side of the rectangles (because the triangles will sit on top, like a roof). You can also make these houses larger, but this is a general guide.
- **Glue or tape**
- **Crayons, markers, or other decorative materials**

INSTRUCTIONS:

1. Cut your paper or fabric into 25 rectangles and 25 triangles.

2. Fold the rectangles in half to make a square with the ends creating an opening at the top.

3. Glue or tape two sides so you create a "pocket" open at the top.

4. Glue or tape the triangle to the front of the paper/fabric to make the roof of the home.

5. Decorate each home however you'd like. (Letting your children or grandchildren color each house adds a special touch that will bring a smile to your face each year when you take your Advent banner out!)

6. Hang each "home" along your banner/garland from end to end. (You can use tape, glue, or even a stapler to attach each house to your ribbon.)

7. Create a small figurine or symbol out of paper or cloth to move from each home's "pocket" every day. A star is a good choice as it represents the star that led the wise men to Bethlehem, just as you and your family will journey to Bethlehem over the next twenty-five days.

8. Hang up your uniquely beautiful creation, and enjoy it every day as you use it to count down to Christmas.

9. Pick a time each day that you and the members of your home will move the star (or figurine) along the banner to represent moving closer to the coming of Jesus.

DAY 2

ARRIVAL
of Advent

In his writings, the prophet Isaiah proclaimed the coming of the Savior. Isaiah's prophecies are referenced many times in this devotional because they point directly to the coming of Jesus as a baby.

Therefore the Lord himself will give you a sign.
Look, the young woman is with child and shall bear a son,
and shall name him Immanuel.
– Isaiah 7:14

One of the many incredible things about the Bible is that the Lord offers multiple confirmations of prophecies throughout Scripture. It's fascinating to see how many came true centuries after they were written down. Looking at how many Old Testament prophecies were fulfilled by Jesus can give us the confidence we need to trust what the Lord says.

In the case of Isaiah 7:14, Matthew tells us that the "young woman," or "virgin," did indeed give birth to a Son, and that baby was Jesus.

All this took place to fulfill what had been spoken by the Lord through the prophet: "Look, the virgin shall conceive and bear a son, and they shall name him Emmanuel."
– Matthew 1:22-23

Isaiah believed the Savior would one day be born of a virgin. Matthew lived to see Isaiah's prophecy come true.

In Isaiah 7:14, the NRSV Bible says "Look," while many other translations use the word "Behold." That word often marks something significant, so it's our clue to pay attention to what comes next.

Our Savior would come to earth, and He would be called Immanuel, which means, "God with us."

The fulfillment of Isaiah's prophecy was a message of encouragement. God would not abandon His people—He would be with them, no matter what. But as it turned out, "Immanuel" meant far more than that. The Son to be born would be God Himself, come to earth to dwell among His people, "God with us."

Matthew spells *Immanuel* as "Emmanuel" because he is quoting the Greek translation of the Old Testament. Both spellings carry the same meaning.

Jesus's very name, Immanuel, told those around Him that God was near. Finally, this God that might have seemed distant or difficult to imagine to some was among us, close to us so that He could draw us closer to Him..

In a dark room, you can light one candle, and the light will reach the four corners, illuminating everything in its path. However, the closer you are to the light, the more the light will be all that you can see.

Advent Activity

To contemplate the message of Isaiah 7:14 and Matthew 1:22–23, alone or together as a family, go to your Living Room and turn out all the lights.

Grab one candle, and light it in the center of the room.

Notice how far the light reaches.

Sit far away, and see how the light fills the space. You know what happens when you are far from a lit candle and you only have a little bit of the light? You can see more of the things around you. It's dark in the room, but you can still make out so much because of the light shining at a distance.

Now move closer to the lit candle, and notice how much more of the light you can see. Notice how, when you are close to the candle, you can't see very much around you. It's difficult to focus on anything but the light, isn't it?

This "light" in our lives should be our Savior, Immanuel, God with us.

This is how it ought to be with the Lord. We should want to be so close to Jesus—so close to Immanuel—that we see His light at its brightest. The Lord wants for us to be so close to Him that His light is all that we can see.

He is all that matters, and He has arrived.

The author and minister Matthew Henry once wrote, "By the light of nature we see God as a God above us; by the light of the law we see him as a God against us; but by the light of the Gospel we see Him as Immanuel, God with us."

Advent Prayer

God, thank You for Your Word. Thank You for the scriptures that tell us about the coming of our Savior. Thank You for sending us a Messiah who would be with us now and for eternity. Thank you for the light He is in our lives and how He illuminates the path You would have us follow.

DAY 3

AWAKEN
to Advent

Mary was the first person in the entire universe to be awakened to who Jesus was. But when the angel Gabriel arrived with his message, she had questions, as any human would!

First of all, an angel coming to you is enough to put anyone on notice. But then, Gabriel told her something so outlandish—

that she would bear a child even though she had never been with a man, and that this child would be the Messiah.

It would have been completely understandable if anyone literally passed out on hearing a message like that one, straight from the angel's mouth.

But while Mary questioned, she also immediately listened.

The angel said to her, "Do not be afraid, Mary, for you have found favor with God. And now, you will conceive in your womb and bear a son, and you will name him Jesus. He will be great, and will be called the Son of the Most High, and the Lord God will give to him the throne of his ancestor David. He will reign over the house of Jacob forever, and of his kingdom there will be no end."

Mary said to the angel, "How can this be, since I am a virgin?"

The angel said to her, "The Holy Spirit will come upon you, and the power of the Most High will overshadow you; therefore the child to be born will be holy; he will be called Son of God. And now, your relative Elizabeth in her old age has also conceived a son; and this is the sixth month for her who was said to be barren. For nothing will be impossible with God." Then Mary said, "Here am I, the servant of the Lord; let it be with me according to your word."

Then the angel departed from her.

– Luke 1: 30-38

First, Mary was told she will give birth to the Son of God, and then she hears that her cousin Elizabeth, who is much too old to bear children, is pregnant. Gabriel's message was clear: if the Lord can do this for Elizabeth, then He can surely create a child in Mary's womb!

He even makes a point to say, "Nothing will be impossible with God." With this promise, Mary pivoted immediately to obedience and trust. She believed the angel and welcomed his miraculous news into her life with open arms.

In Luke, Mary visits her cousin Elizabeth. Perhaps she needed to see for herself. *Was Elizabeth really with child? Could this be?*

It was so. Mary saw it with her own two eyes. And her response is a beautiful prayer that echoes the praises of the Psalms:

*And Mary said, "My soul magnifies the Lord, and my spirit rejoices
in God my Savior, for he has looked with favor on the lowliness of
his servant. Surely, from now on all generations will call me blessed;
for the Mighty One has done great things for me,
and holy is his name. His mercy is for those who fear him from
generation to generation. He has shown strength with his arm; he
has scattered the proud in the thoughts of their hearts.
He has brought down the powerful from their thrones, and lifted
up the lowly; he has filled the hungry with good things, and sent the
rich away empty. He has helped his servant Israel, in remembrance
of his mercy, according to the promise he made to our ancestors,
to Abraham and to his descendants forever."*
– Luke 1:46-55

In that moment, Mary knew her place in history would
be profound. She was grateful to the Lord for bestowing this
honor upon her—so grateful that her thankfulness bubbles up
to the surface, and she proclaims these words of praise to the
Lord.

When Mary began her prayer by saying "my soul magnifies
the Lord," she was structuring her praise off of Psalm 34:1–3,
which says, "I will bless the Lord at all times; his praise shall
continually be in my mouth. <u>My soul</u> makes its boast in the Lord;

let the humble hear and be glad. O <u>magnify the Lord</u> with me, and let us exalt his name together" (emphasis added).

Mary demonstrated how important it is to allow our thankfulness to the Lord to rise from our hearts to our lips and spill out in praise.

The prominent nineteenth-century preacher Charles Spurgeon said, "His praise shall continually be in my mouth, not in my heart merely, but in my mouth too. . . . If we continually rolled this dainty morsel under our tongue, the bitterness of daily affliction would be swallowed up in joy. God deserves blessing with the heart, and extolling with the mouth—good thoughts in the closet, and good words in the world."

What thankfulness have you kept inside? What gratefulness have you left in your prayer closet?

Advent Activity

The practice of gratitude is such an important one, not only for your soul, but also for the souls around you.

As you gather as a family in your Living Room today, take a few moments to go around the room and share what you are thankful for. In this way, your home will be filled with your own psalms of praise for what the Lord has done in your lives.

If you feel inclined, sing together as a family (or play for all to listen) the song "To God Be the Glory." This hymn holds a beautiful message of thanksgiving to the Lord, for the gift of His Son and for the ongoing, wonderful work He does in our lives.

Reflect as a family on Mary's prayer and what must have been going through her mind and her heart as she was awakened to who Jesus was and her place in His story.

Our thankfulness to God should be a song for others to hear, that they might hear about the Lord and His goodness. Mary knew this, and it is why she praised with her lips.

Advent Prayer

Lord, what magnificent things You have brought into our lives! You loved us enough to send Your Son to this earth to save us, You have given us family and friends to share life with, and You continually pour out blessings in millions of ways. Thank You for Your provision, and especially for loving us so well.

DAY 4

ANOINTING
of Advent

The writer of Hebrews quotes Psalm 45:6–7 to show that Jesus's anointing is greater than that of a mere prophet, priest, or king. It is beyond all others. There is nothing like it. Jesus has been placed above every other creature or thing ever created!

But of the Son he says, "Your throne, O God, is forever and ever, and the righteous scepter is the scepter of your kingdom. You have loved righteousness and hated wickedness; therefore God, your God, has anointed you with the oil of gladness beyond your companions."
– Hebrews 1:8-9

The influential South African theologian, mission organizer, and writer Andrew Murray once wrote,

> That Spirit [the Holy Spirit] was to Him the oil of joy, the joy that had been set before him, the joy of His crowning day when He saw of the travail of His soul. An anointing above His fellows, for there was none like Him; God gave Him the Spirit without measure. And yet for His fellows, His redeemed, whom, as Head, He had made members of His body. They become partakers of His anointing and His joy. As He said, "The Lord hath anointed Me to give the oil of joy."

Though Jesus's anointing as Messiah is unique and will never be repeated, Jesus chose to share His anointing with us. He chose to give us the Holy Spirit. As Murray pointed out, this allows us to share in His joy.

Think about that for a moment. Jesus came to earth to be anointed by His Father as the Savior of the world, the most preeminent being in our entire universe, and then Jesus chose to share His blessings with us. He wanted to make a way for us to be with Him and His Father forever.

What a blessing! Jesus came as a gift to this world, but He came to bring us personal gifts as well—the gift of the Spirit and the gift of eternal life.

Advent Prayer

Jesus, thank You for sharing Your anointing with us. The Holy Spirit in our lives is a wonderful gift. He is our faithful guide as we walk with You daily, bringing us joy, no matter what life brings our way. Help me to be an ambassador of this joy as I share the gospel with others.

Advent Activity

To practice this love for one another and teach us about the anointing Jesus shared with us, we can pray out loud for the loved ones in our home.

It was common in Hebrew homes for guests to be anointed with oil. Today, if you have some oil (such as olive oil) in your home, have it available as you gather in the Living Room. Ask each person to have a prayerful spirit as you pray for one another out loud.

As each person prays, have them dip their fingertip in oil and place it on the forehead of the person they are praying for.

As you anoint one another with oil, pray for the Lord's protection and thank Him for His wisdom to protect their mind, or thank the Lord for this person's wisdom.

You can also place oil on someone's palms and ask the Lord to guide their hands as they work each day, or thank the Lord for the work He has given them to do.

DAY 5

ADORATION
of Advent

The privilege of the believer in Christ is to adore Him forever. We have been given such astounding gifts from the Lord that we cannot help but adore Him.

In fact, that was the response of the wise men who journeyed from the East to find the newborn King of the Jews. They knew he was no ordinary king, because "they knelt down and paid him homage" (Matthew 2:11). Awakened to who Jesus was, they worshipped him.

As we journey toward Christmas this Advent season, that's our goal: to bow down and worship the King. And He is worthy of our worship. There is no sacrifice too great, no gesture too grand. Jesus deserves it all! As the book of Hebrews reminds us, "our God is a consuming fire."

Therefore, since we are receiving a kingdom that cannot be shaken, let us give thanks, by which we offer to God an acceptable worship with reverence and awe; for indeed our God is a consuming fire.
– Hebrews 12:28-29

When you gain Jesus, you are overcome with thanksgiving and joy. He is holy, righteous, and good. He is perfect in every way. He loves us with such an unfailing love that He has given us eternal life in His kingdom.

Charles Spurgeon said, "Is it not wonderful that it should be written, 'We are receiving a kingdom'? What a gift to receive! This is a divine gift; we have received, not a pauper's pension, but a kingdom that cannot be moved."

It's so easy to anticipate Christmas presents with expectant feelings and excited thoughts.

You see presents wrapped with your name on the tag, and you can't help but wonder what might be inside. But the joy of unwrapping presents is so fleeting. You open it to realize what lies inside is no longer a mystery. The thrill of anticipation is gone in an instant.

Sometimes this anticipation gives way to delight, if the gift is something you've been hoping for, or it can be followed by tremendous disappointment, if you unwrap something you don't really care for.

Our gifts here on earth are not of the lasting kind, but the gift of God's kingdom is never ending. It is for all who know Jesus to enjoy in this age and in the age to come, forever without end. The beautiful thing about God's kingdom is that its vastness can never fully be taken in. We learn about it daily as we walk with Jesus, and we discover new aspects of the kingdom all the time.

This kind of gift is the most fascinating gift you could ever receive.

The shine will never dim. The last page will never be turned. The look will never go out of style.

You belong, you are needed, you are loved, and you are wanted in God's kingdom.

The Lord's kingdom and all that is within it is yours for the taking, as a child of God.

Spurgeon had it right: "What a gift to receive!"

When we unwrap such a gift, the only response is awe, as the writer of Hebrews tells us. We stand before our great God, who is like an all-consuming fire.

But just as fire destroy things, it also clears the way for rebirth. Consuming is such a perfect word for what it does. Because of Jesus's sacrifice, if we have trusted Him as our Lord and Savior, we do not have to fear judgment. Instead, we stand ready to be consumed by God's love. The Lord's love for us is all consuming.

Advent Prayer

Lord, thank You for giving us the gift of Your kingdom as believers in Christ. Thank You that we get to inherit treasure beyond anything this world can offer. We stand in awe of who You are and that you came down to the earth for us. Thank You for consuming us with Your love.

Advent Activity

If you have a fireplace in your home, gather your family around that space today. For many people, this will be in the Living Room.

If you so choose, light the fire. If you do not have a fireplace, light a candle for the family to sit around.

Read Hebrews 12:28–29 aloud.

Explain the difference between our gifts here on earth, and the gift of the kingdom Jesus came to give us.

Talk with your family about the all-consuming nature of the Lord and the gift of salvation He came to give us.

As you each look at the fire and think about its properties and the warmth it is bringing to your home, have each person share how the Lord has been "all consuming" this year.

What has God done this year to bring awe to your life? What part of His kingdom became more real to you this year?

CELEBRATING ADVENT IN THE

Dining Room

DAY 6
ANTICIPATION
of Advent

As Luke tells the story of Jesus's birth, He uses the word "holy" quite a few times.

✦

The angel said to her, "The Holy Spirit will come upon you, and the power of the Most High will overshadow you; therefore the child to be born will be holy; he will be called Son of God."

– Luke 1:35

Our Savior would come to us as a child, but not just any child—He would radically change our lives. He would be holy, and through His holiness, allow holiness into our lives.

To be holy is to be set apart, uncommon, sacred. Gabriel, the angel who appeared to Mary, told her how special her Son would be. He would be set apart from every other human, unlike any person who would ever be on the earth or in heaven. He would be the Son of God, fully divine, but also come as a child, fully human. What a concept for Mary to try and wrap her mind around!

In the Greek translation of Exodus 40:35, the same word translated "overshadow" here in Luke's gospel is used to describe God's presence settling upon the tent. God the Son was coming to dwell with His people, and similar to the way a shadow offers shade to the ground, the Lord signified His upcoming arrival to Mary through the shade of His presence.

Just as Jesus was set apart for the kingdom work He was given to do, so too do we set apart areas of our home for celebrations. The Dining Room, in particular, is often saved for holidays and special occasions, so it's a wonderful place for gathering together to reflect on today's scripture.

When we set the table in anticipation of our guests, especially when we're creating a space to celebrate Jesus

together, we are setting apart a special place to dine—making it holy through that act of celebration.

Advent Prayer

God, thank You for sending us a Savior who is holy—a Savior who is sacred and set apart, worthy of our worship and adoration. Thank You for this time to be set apart and to celebrate with the ones we love the most. Help us to remember your holiness and sacredness, and help us to reflect that holiness in our own lives.

Advent Activity

Set your table in the Dining Room with the placemats, plates, and silverware you normally reserve for special occasions.

Print the sheet music for the hymn "O Holy Night" and place a copy at each setting, or use the page as the placemat.

Down the center of the table, run a strand of white Christmas lights or place candles up and down the center of the table. When everyone is seated, dim the lights and turn on the strand of lights or light the candles.

By dimming the main lights in the Dining Room and lighting the centerpiece, we allow the room to be "overshadowed," creating a unique atmosphere in which to reflect on our passage for the day.

Sing "O Holy Night" together as a family by the glow of the light in the room, thinking about the lyrics as you sing them. (You can also choose to play your favorite version of the hymn and simply listen quietly.)

DAY 7
ARRIVAL
of Advent

Brennan Manning once wrote, "Christmas means that God has given us nothing less than Himself, and His name is Jesus Christ. Be unwilling to settle for anything less. . . . Don't come with a thimble when God has nothing less to give you than the ocean of Himself."

This season is, most importantly, about God arriving to be with His people.

Isaiah prophesied long before Jesus was born, but He told God's people that the Messiah was coming and that He would be the Savior of the world.

For a child has been born for us, a son given to us; authority rests upon his shoulders; and he is named Wonderful Counselor, Mighty God, Everlasting Father, Prince of Peace.
— Isaiah 9:6

Jesus would be the Wonderful Counselor, Mighty God, Everlasting Father, and Prince of Peace.

Because there is so much to unpack in these attributes, we're going to look at two of these wonderful titles today (and we will look at the other two on Day 22).

JESUS AS EVERLASTING FATHER

The Hebrew translation here is *Abi'ad* which means "The Father of Eternity." This description of Jesus as a father does not imply that He is God the Father, but rather that as the Messiah, He would care for His people, as a good father cares for his children.

A father protects his children when they are in danger. A father comforts his children when they are in distress. A father has compassion for his children when they are in need. Jesus is this kind of father.

An earthly father who loves well is a wonderful blessing that can point us to the love of Jesus, yet our Lord's love is exponentially greater than anything we can experience here on earth.

Fathers and mothers alike have special insight into the love of God because they understand the depth of love they have for their own children, but God's capacity for love exceeds our own. If we love our children this much, how much more must the Father love us?

Jesus our Savior protects us and loves us as only a father can love his very own children.

What a gift it is to know you are loved like this and you are chosen!

JESUS AS PRINCE OF PEACE

Peace.

In Hebrew, it's the word *shalom*. Even if you can't read a bit of Hebrew, chances are you've come across this word before. It means many things, but shalom is more than just the absence of war; it is wholeness and well-being.

Isaiah promised that the Savior to come would bring shalom with Him—the kind of peace we all long for.

But the longing is not enough. Whether you experience internal wars of the heart and soul or external wars of conflict, calm can seem always out of reach. The answer is to turn to the source of peace. Isaiah showed us that Jesus was the ultimate source of peace and thus by saying Jesus was a prince, this title Prince of Peace was a divine title.

Those of steadfast mind you keep in peace—
in peace because they trust in you.
– Isaiah 26:3

Peace. It's the atmosphere we want to live in all year long, but especially during Advent, and it's one of the gifts Jesus brings in His arrival.

Jesus our Savior calms the storms and silences the wars around us.

Advent Activity

The Dining Room, in many homes, is a place of tranquility.

This is the space where you gather around a beautifully prepared table and pray before a specially prepared meal.

This year, as you set your table for a family meal, put little place cards at each seat with a prayer you have written for the family member or friend who will sit in that seat.

You can also ask other family members and friends to do the same for the others at the table.

Write a prayer asking the Lord Jesus to reveal Himself as their Everlasting Father or their Prince of Peace when they most need the reminder during the coming year.

Remind your loved ones that Jesus is a gift given to us this Advent season. He cares for us as a Father and brings us peace beyond measure.

Take some time at the beginning or the end of the meal to quietly read your cards.

What a gift of tranquility!

What is it you most need this Advent season?

Is it the care of an Everlasting Father or the calm that only the Prince of Peace can bring? Perhaps you need both during this busy season.

After you think about your own life, think about those around you. How can you pray for your family and friends to experience Jesus as the Everlasting Father and the Prince of Peace?

Sharing who Jesus is to us, and who we long for Him to be for others, is a great gift we can give this Advent season.

Advent Prayer

Lord, thank You for giving us the gift of Jesus, who cares for us as a Father and who brings us the greatest peace we will ever know. Thank You for the gift of family and friends, with whom we can celebrate this season.

DAY 8

AWAKEN
to Advent

Though Mary was the first to learn that the Messiah was coming into the world, Joseph, her soon-to-be husband, was the second to know about Jesus. But he knew he couldn't be the father, since he and Mary had never been intimate.

Matthew tells us that Joseph was a good man who wanted to divorce Mary quietly. He didn't see a way he could stay with her, since it appeared she was carrying another man's child. But it only appeared that way. Mary was, of course, telling Joseph the truth about her pregnancy, but it took a special messenger to convince Joseph. An angel of the Lord appeared to Joseph in a dream and corroborated Mary's story.

*When Joseph awoke from sleep, he did as the
angel of the Lord commanded him; he took her as his wife,
but had no marital relations with her until she had
borne a son; and he named him Jesus.*
– Matthew 1:24-25

Euthymius, a fifth-century monk who lived in the Holy Land, said this of Joseph: "Why did he so easily trust the dream in so great a matter? Because the angel revealed to him the thought of his own heart, for he understood that the messenger must have come from God, for God alone knows the thoughts of the heart."

God alone knows your heart.

The scripture tells us Joseph planned to divorced Mary "quietly." In other words, no one yet knew what Mary had told him or what he had thought to do. No one knew he was doubting Mary's story. When the angel of the Lord appeared to him, though, he knew that both the child and the angel had to

be from God. Who else could have known what he was thinking and considering in his heart?

This is when Joseph was awakened to the reality that the child growing in Mary's womb was Jesus, and Joseph would have a place in the incredible story God was writing.

Scripture doesn't tell us what Joseph was thinking once he came to this realization. Matthew doesn't record anything Joseph says. We do not get to see what it looked like to have his mind blown or for him to come to a full realization of the Messiah.

But the Bible does tell us that Joseph acted with a sense of urgency. When the Lord spoke through His angel, Joseph immediately obeyed. There was no more hesitating, no more wondering, no more questioning. The Lord spoke, and Joseph got to work.

How often do we hear from the Lord in our everyday lives yet question what He's told us to do? It's easy to hesitate when He isn't standing right in front of us. It's easy to question God when

He hasn't put you in a deep sleep, given you a miraculous angel-dream, and spoken so profoundly.

Maybe there is something the Lord has been showing you repeatedly, and now you know it's time to acknowledge this as His leading.

Is there a prayer to pray, a task to execute, a question to ask, a heart to seek? What is the Lord prompting you to do right now? **If you are unsure of His voice, take some time to quietly seek His heart in prayer today.**

Please know you are not alone in your questioning. We all question the mark of His hand in our lives and the prompting He places on our hearts. It's a natural and human reaction to sometimes question, just as it must have been for Joseph when Mary first shared the story of her pregnancy with him.

Advent Prayer

God, thank You for Your Word, which tells us about this moment in time You had with Joseph. Thank You for giving him the wisdom to obey You—and to obey You quickly. Thank You for the example Joseph set. May we all react as quickly as him when You call to us.

Advent Activity

Grab some paper and cut out one heart shape for each person who will join you for dinner tonight.

As you set the table for dinner, place a paper heart and a pen at each setting.

Before you begin eating, read Matthew 1:24–25 to your family. Explain how Joseph had doubts he kept inside his heart about the incredible news Mary shared with him.

Then ask each member of your family to write down a doubt, a fear, or a desire held so deep within their heart that only the Lord knows about it.

Next, have each person gathered write a prayer to the Lord on that heart, asking Him to make His presence evident this Advent season, so that there can be no way of doubting His work in their lives and His goodness.

Follow up your discussion by sharing how Joseph immediately listened to the Lord and did as He commanded. Encourage your family members to do the same in each of their own lives: to immediately obey the Lord when He is leading.

ANOINTING
of Advent

It is not enough to merely know of Jesus's arrival and be awakened to who He is; we must also recognize and affirm His anointing as the Savior of the world, the Messiah. This recognition of His anointing was what set Him apart from every other man on earth.

DINING ROOM

He is the image of the invisible God, the firstborn of all creation; for in him all things in heaven and on earth were created, things visible and invisible, whether thrones or dominions or rulers or powers— all things have been created through him and for him. He himself is before all things, and in him all things hold together.
— Colossians 1:15-17

What an impactful statement about who Jesus is!

If you've ever wondered what life was about or where history is headed, this passage gives the answer: Jesus. It's all about Him. It always has been and always will be.

HE IS:

The image of the invisible God

The firstborn of all creation

Before all things

IN HIM:

All things were created, in heaven and on earth, visible and invisible

All things were created THROUGH Him

All things were created FOR Him

All things hold together

Paul packed all of that into three tiny verses in Colossians. We could spend a lifetime studying this one passage, but today we'll look at two of the phrases used to describe Jesus:

THE IMAGE OF THE INVISIBLE GOD

The people of Paul's time were searching for a Savior to bring them so many things, but one of the things they longed for was peace. To find peace with God, they needed to find forgiveness, and the basis for all forgiveness was—and is—in Jesus.

When God created human beings, He made them in His image (Genesis 1:27). That means we were made like God, but more than that, we were made to reflect His image to one another. Now we know that none of us even comes close to reflecting God perfectly. But Jesus does. He is the image of the invisible God, the perfect picture of who the Father is.

Paul is saying the forgiveness that comes through Jesus is forgiveness directly from the Father Himself.

Whatever we imagined God to be like, Jesus showed us that in the flesh. What a fantastic gift!

THE FIRSTBORN OF ALL CREATION & BEFORE ALL THINGS

Paul is also showing us that Jesus is the absolute Supreme Being through his juxtaposition of Christ with creation; "the firstborn of all creation; for in him all things in heaven and on earth were created, things visible and invisible."

When Paul writes that Jesus is the "firstborn of all creation," He doesn't mean that Jesus was the first thing God made. Jesus is God and was there in the beginning with God. Instead, Paul's talking about status. In the ancient world, a firstborn son was given special responsibilities, a greater inheritance, and a place of leadership within the family. Jesus has been given this status over all creation.

He is the only #1 there has ever been, or ever will be.

What has been your view of the invisible God? How have you pictured Jesus within the context of creation?

The believers in Colossae who received Paul's letter would have known the story of creation from the book of Genesis.

So God created humankind in his image,
in the image of God he created them.
– Genesis 1:27

Advent Activity

When you set the dinner table today, add a mirror to each place setting. If you do not have enough mirrors, put some mirrors on the table to be passed around and shared.

As you take some time as a family to pray for your meal, thank the Lord for creating you in His image and for loving you just as you are.

Instruct your dinner guests to take a few moments to look at themselves in their mirrors.

This exercise will not be an easy one, but it is very worthwhile.

Ask them to close their eyes and reflect on the uniqueness of Christ based on Colossians 1:15–17 as you read it over them.

After a few moments, have them open their eyes. Then remind them what Genesis 1:27 says about how we have been created in the image of God. We were made to be like Him, and one day, because of Christ, we will be.

Ask each dinner guest to look in the mirror and pray a prayer of thanksgiving to the Lord for their lives. Remind them to ask the Lord to continue to show them His amazing purpose for their lives.

If we are searching for the unseen God, the God who says we are created in His image—how many times have we looked in the mirror and missed seeing His creation?

This is not to say that our image perfectly mirrors God's—not at all. But when you look at yourself, you're looking at God's creation. You're looking at someone He loves, someone He came to this earth to save and to give eternal life. You may not be able to physically see Him, but you can see His handiwork in your eyes.

The Spirit is at work making us more like Christ, closer to His image, and we have this promise: when Jesus returns for His followers, we will become like Him (1 Corinthians 15:49). Then we'll reflect God's image perfectly, just as we were made to do.

Advent Prayer

Lord, thank You for creating us in Your image. Thank You for sending Your Son to this earth to become human and embody things we can relate to as humans, but also be a Supreme Being that would come to save us and show us what Your perfect image looks like. Thank you for Your anointing. Help us find ways every day to see Your anointing in our own lives and be thankful for it as we try to reflect Your image in our lives.

DAY 10
ADORATION
of Advent

We find in the story of Jesus's birth the same humility with which He approached everything during His time on earth.

In the book of Philippians, we are instructed to imitate the humility of Christ. Though He is fully God, He came to this earth as a human and was obedient to His Father in heaven.

*Therefore God also highly exalted him and gave him
the name that is above every name, so that at the name of Jesus
every knee should bend, in heaven and on earth and under the
earth, and every tongue should confess that Jesus Christ is Lord,
to the glory of God the Father.*
– Philippians 2:9-11

The Lord gave Jesus the name above every other name.

Jesus as the name ABOVE all names is for the betterment of humankind.

Jesus as the name ABOVE all names benefits the entire world.

And as the name ABOVE all names, He has extended His blessings upon us, for our eternal betterment and benefit, even after the world as we know it passes away.

What other god or person could have ever had the same things said of them? This is why He is ABOVE all things.

As Philippians reminds us, because of the name of Jesus, everyone will worship Him with knees bent and heads bowed in reverence to our Savior. And everyone who worships Jesus will confess that He is Lord. This will be our expression of adoration for who He is.

When the Wise Men visited baby Jesus, Matthew 2:11 recounts that "they knelt down and paid him homage." They were among the first to do what Philippians tells us everyone will one day do: bend their knees in worship to the King. They were showing their adoration to Jesus.

When the shepherds visited baby Jesus, Luke 2:20 says, "The shepherds returned, glorifying and praising God for all they had heard and seen, as it had been told them." They were showing adoration by speaking about Jesus publicly.

Advent Activity

When you set the Dining Room table for dinner tonight, put a card or piece of paper next to each place setting with today's scripture, Philippians 2:9–11, handwritten or typed on it.

As you sit down to dinner tonight, have each person take a turn reading the verses out loud to the others at the table.

It will be repetitive for sure, but this is one way we can memorize and meditate on what the Lord is teaching us through His Word. Ask each person to reflect on the name of Jesus as they read and listen to others. Ask them to think about their posture of prayer and how they can spend time simply adoring the Lord this season.

If everyone is willing, when you finish reading the scripture (at the beginning or at the end of the meal), have everyone kneel next to their Dining Room chair. Have someone offer up a prayer of thanksgiving to the Lord for the name of Jesus and all that His name means to us today.

These verses show us how to worship the Lord in our prayer life: by bowing down in adoration to Jesus and by speaking the truth of who Jesus is.

Advent Prayer

Jesus, what a sweet name: a name that brings us so much calm and joy. Thank You for a time set apart to reflect on Your entrance into this world, the act that would bring us salvation. May our actions and words show that we love You and adore You.

CELEBRATING ADVENT IN THE

Kitchen

DAY 11

ANTICIPATION
of Advent

The book of Isaiah is packed full of promises of the coming Messiah. Isaiah foretold many of the things God would do for His people through the birth and ministry of Christ, and therefore became a source of hope and encouragement for the people of Judah in his day and people all over for many years to come.

We can imagine many other people thought Isaiah had lost his mind. Many, though, probably hoped he was exactly right.

The prophet Isaiah describes the future kingdom of the Lord:

A shoot shall come out from the stump of Jesse, and a branch shall grow out of his roots. The spirit of the Lord shall rest on him, the spirit of wisdom and understanding, the spirit of counsel and might, the spirit of knowledge and the fear of the Lord. His delight shall be in the fear of the Lord. He shall not judge by what his eyes see, or decide by what his ears hear; but with righteousness he shall judge the poor, and decide with equity for the meek of the earth.

– Isaiah 11:1-4

This was a reference to Jesus's royal lineage as a descendant of David, but it also describes Jesus coming to earth as a fruit-bearing sign of the Lord. Jesus would come possessed with the Spirit of the Lord; He would have wisdom and complete understanding. He would be a counselor, and He would be mighty and full of knowledge.

Then Isaiah says Jesus would not judge by what He sees with His eyes, or what He hears with His ears. He would decide things with His heart of righteousness and meekness.

What a great picture and reminder of the equity we have in Christ. With Jesus, there are no unfair dealings, and no one is above the law. He didn't come only for the rich or for the poor. He didn't come just for the Jews, but also welcomed Gentiles. Jesus isn't partial to anyone.

When the baby Jesus came to this world, He came to save you specifically, but He also came to save everyone else.

Advent Prayer

Jesus, thank You for being the shoot from the stump of Jesse. Thank You for coming to save us. Thank You for loving each of us perfectly and for bringing a kingdom where justice will be perfect. Thank You for your kindness and goodness and mercy. Please continue to grow these traits within us so when we are outside of this home, people know we are Yours by the fruit we bear in our lives.

Advent Activity

Today, as you work in your Kitchen to prepare meals and snacks for your family, create a platter of your family's favorite fruit.

Grapes, apples, and bananas, among other fruits, are often available in grocery stores in December.

Bring your family together for a snack time or at the beginning of a meal, and explain to them what bearing fruit means. Use the fruits you have picked as examples.

Example: When this banana was picked from a tree, the banana proved both what kind of tree it was, a banana tree, and that it was alive and healthy, because it grew bananas.

When these grapes were picked from a vine, the grapes proved that the vine was a healthy grapevine.

In Isaiah's prophecy, "the stump of Jesse" is a reference to the royal line of King David, Jesse's son, which was thought to be a "stump" because there had been no kings from David's family in centuries. People thought that family tree was dead and wouldn't bear any fruit.

But then Jesus was born, descended from David, the one who would sit on His throne, just as God promised. He is the shoot that grew from the stump, and he bore all the fruits that Isaiah described.

In the same manner, when we as God's children show His love and His kindness, we bear witness, we bear fruit, that we are Christians.

The Savior we anticipate at Christmas is a Savior who is bearing fruit through each of us as His children. He is the tree with many branches, and we're the fruit springing forth from His tree of promises.

When we believe in Jesus Christ, we walk as people who will then bear fruit to who He is.

Now, bring your family's attention to the three different fruits you have chosen.

Isaiah reminds us in chapter 11 verse 4 that Jesus is coming to "decide with equity."

Explain that *equity* means being "fair or impartial."

The Savior came to earth so everyone could have a FAIR share of His kingdom. No one will be taken advantage of, and no one will be treated as a second-class citizen. He came so that all may know Him and live in His blessing. He doesn't judge each of us based on a different scale, but to the same one. When we come to Jesus Christ as our Lord, we are each heirs to His love and kingdom, which knows no injustice.

Ask one of your family members to give everyone an EQUAL share of the fruit to portray our equity in Christ.

DAY 12

ARRIVAL
of Advent

When Isaiah was predicting the arrival of Jesus, he was giving us all a sign of the fullness we would soon experience in our hearts. He was giving us a sneak preview of the antidote for all of our worries and fears. Our minds and hearts would soon know the fullness of Christ.

But when the fullness of time had come, God sent his Son,
born of a woman, born under the law.
– Galatians 4:4

The fullness of time.

What does the fullness of time really mean?

The time had come for Jesus to be born. This was a time set by the Lord for when He knew the Savior would enter the world. He had predestined this moment in history.

Paul uses the same word in Colossians 2:9 when he says, "For in him the whole fullness of deity dwells bodily."

The Bible often has "fullness" and "dwell" coupled together. When the Lord is filling you up, he is also dwelling—or taking up residence—in your heart, and mind, and body, and soul.

The totality mentioned here implies completeness. Not only did God plan Jesus's birth for the perfect time, but Jesus coming to earth would bring completeness to mankind. It also means there was no gap. There was nothing lacking from beginning to end.

The fullness of Christ in the fullness of time. Think about when you pour yourself some hot apple cider at Christmastime. You fill your mug and as you do, the cider pushes out all of the

air; all of the <u>empty</u> (air) contents move out of the mug as the <u>full</u> (cider) contents come into the mug.

This is what Jesus's arrival on the scene did for all of mankind.

Jesus pushed out empty worship, pushed out vacancy in people's hearts, and pushed out the loneliness and longing in the lives of those around Him, and filled all of that space with Himself, with the fullness of His presence.

His arrival left no gaps between God and us and made complete our relationship with Him, so that we could experience Him fully.

Jesus was all anyone would ever need.

Advent Prayer

Lord, thank You for Your ability to fill every void we have in our hearts. Thank You for sending Jesus right when the world needed Him. Thank You for loving us enough to send Your Son to complete the incomplete world we live in. We are forever grateful that You have chosen to dwell with us.

Advent Activity

While in your Kitchen today, put this concept of fullness to practice by making your family and friends a wonderful, hot holiday drink. An example from this lesson is hot apple cider.

Buying the apple cider of your choice is always an option; however, an easy recipe for hot apple cider requires four ingredients:

- 2–4 cinnamon sticks
- 1 tsp whole allspice
- 1 tsp whole cloves
- 1 jar of unsweetened apple juice

(if you want the cider sweeter, add 1/3 cup brown sugar and boil/stir until it dissolves)

Boil the apple juice on the stove with the cinnamon sticks, allspice, and cloves in the pot.

When the juice becomes aromatic and has reached a steaming temperature, scoop the spices out, and pour some cider to enjoy.

When you pour the cider into mugs, discuss Galatians 4:4 with your family. Describe how Jesus came to earth when it was the "fullness of time," both at just the right moment and in a way that allows us to experience the fullness of Jesus.

Ask your family and friends to think about how pouring the cider into our mugs demonstrates the "fullness of time."

DAY 13

AWAKEN
to Advent

The coming of the Messiah was anticipated, but because no one knew exactly when He might arrive, His entrance to this world felt very sudden to many—including certain shepherds who were just minding their own business, tending their flocks.

In our own lives, as with the shepherds in fields outside of Bethlehem, we can be minding our own business, doing our everyday mundane tasks, and the Lord drops in like a lightning bolt.

Out of nowhere, an angel of the Lord appeared to the shepherds, tending their flock, and told them that Christ had been born.

But the angel said to them, "Do not be afraid; for see—I am bringing you good news of great joy for all the people: to you is born this day in the city of David a Savior, who is the Messiah, the Lord. This will be a sign for you: you will find a child wrapped in bands of cloth and lying in a manger." And suddenly there was with the angel a multitude of the heavenly host, praising God and saying, "Glory to God in the highest heaven, and on earth peace among those whom he favors!" When the angels had left them and gone into heaven, the shepherds said to one another, "Let us go now to Bethlehem and see this thing that has taken place, which the Lord has made known to us." So they went with haste and found Mary and Joseph, and the child lying in the manger. When they saw this, they made known what had been told them about this child; and all who heard it were amazed at what the shepherds told them. But Mary treasured all these words and pondered them in her heart. The shepherds returned, glorifying and praising God for all they had heard and seen, as it had been told them.

– Luke 2:11-20

Martin Luther points out when the angel says "to YOU is born this day," WE are meant to receive the wonderful gift of Jesus; He is given for US. Luther said, "This joy was not to remain in Christ, but it shall be to all the people. For this purpose Christ willed to be born, that through him we might be born anew." Though the people didn't know it, Jesus's birth pointed to a new birth for everyone who would trust in Him as their Savior.

Up until this point in biblical history, announcements concerning the Messiah had always been about the future, but the angel tells the shepherds that "this day" the Christ child has been born. It is no longer a hope. It has happened. It is real. They needed to act fast.

So, they listened to the angel's instructions and quickly went to seek out the baby in the manger. "When they saw this, they made known what had been told them about this child" (verse 17).

This was the shepherds' awakening moment. They had seen with their own eyes the Lord Jesus cradled in a feeding trough. They knew who He was, and they could now proclaim the Messiah was finally here. Their reaction to seeing Jesus, as the angel had described, resulted in immediate faith, and they could not hold that truth inside; they had to tell everyone the good news.

This is a perfect example of what should happen to us when we encounter Christ; we should want to tell everyone we can about seeing and experiencing the Messiah.

What a beautiful portrait God gave us by bringing the shepherds to come see Jesus; that Jesus would be to the entire world like a shepherd who cares for his sheep.

⇝ *Advent Prayer* ⇜

Lord, thank You for the story of the shepherds who came to see Jesus. You packed so much in a few short verses; we could spend years unwrapping this scripture. Thank you for watching over us and protecting us just as a shepherd does with his sheep.

Advent Activity

At Christmastime, we often use the candy cane as a symbol of the holiday, but it can also be a teaching tool to share the good news of Jesus.

Today, as you gather family and friends together for a meal in the Kitchen, hand them each a candy cane.

Each element of the candy cane has a specific meaning that ties to the story of the shepherds visiting Jesus.

The white part of the candy cane is a symbol of Jesus's holiness and purity. He is our sinless Savior, and He washes all of our sins away through salvation.

The red part of the candy is a reminder of the blood Jesus would shed on our behalf to offer salvation to the world.

When the candy cane is turned upside down you see a letter J, which represents the name the angel instructed Mary to give to her baby boy: Jesus.

Finally, when the candy cane is upright, it looks a bit like a shepherd's staff. It represents Jesus, the Good Shepherd who watches over us as His flock.

DAY 14
ANOINTING
of Advent

Isaiah told of the fullness that was to come into our lives when Jesus arrived.

The shepherds showed us what happened when they encountered Jesus as Isaiah foretold, and they were never the same.

One of the most beautiful things about believing in Jesus Christ is that you are transformed and made new. Your heart—

indeed, your whole life—is never the same again. The Lord will never leave or forsake you. Nothing can separate you from the love of Jesus.

When we think of Jesus's anointing as the Messiah, the Savior for all people, we think of this deity far above us. Incredibly, through His anointing He came to share an abundant anointing with us.

Through Jesus, we're anointed with the Holy Spirit. God Himself comes to live within us.

As for you, the anointing that you received from him abides in you, and so you do not need anyone to teach you. But as his anointing teaches you about all things, and is true and is not a lie, and just as it has taught you, abide in him.
– 1 John 2:27

The letter we know today as 1 John was written to a church plagued by false teachers. These teachers were attempting to lead true believers astray. John's letter was both a warning about false doctrine and an encouragement. Those who know Christ have the Holy Spirit within them. He is a teacher who can be trusted.

This was John's harkening: listen to your heart. If Jesus is in your heart, then He will not lead you astray.

The word *abide* used in this verse means to "to remain," or "to become as one."

When we put our trust in Jesus as our Lord and Savior, welcoming Him into our hearts, and choose to follow Him, we become one with Him.

Jesus came to earth so that we might be one with Him and the Father in heaven. No separation; dwelling and abiding, remaining as one with us, forever.

Advent Prayer

Jesus, how sweet a gift it is that we can never be separated from You! We can never go back to the people we were before we met You. We are new creations with You in our lives. What a wonderful concept to reflect on this Advent season. Thank You for making us richer through the Holy Spirit, who is at work in our lives.

Advent Activity

As you are in the Kitchen today, get some hot chocolate cocoa powder and a mug of hot water for every member of your household.

Gather your loved ones and read 1 John 2:27 together. Explain how nothing can separate us from the Lord, once He comes to abide with us.

Have someone pour their cocoa powder into their mug of hot water and stir it all together.

Now, after it is all stirred together, ask them to separate the hot water from the powder.

This task is impossible. The powder has become one with the hot water. It has become something new: delicious hot chocolate.

There is no separating the elements; they will remain as one.

This is how it is when we become one with Jesus, when we receive the anointing of the Holy Spirit in our lives.

DAY 15

ADORATION
of Advent

During Jesus's earthly ministry, when the crowds began to follow Him and to believe He was the Messiah they had been waiting for, there were some who weren't happy about it. Some even tried to trick Jesus with tough questions in public, hoping to embarrass Him in front of the crowds.

On one such occasion, a Pharisee stepped forward and asked the Lord about the greatest commandment. Jesus responded by saying,

"You shall love the Lord your God with all your heart, and with all your soul, and with all your mind." This is the greatest and first commandment.
– Matthew 22:37-38

Jesus was saying that the greatest thing anyone can do is to adore the Lord—to love God with all of his or her heart, soul, and mind. We are to love the Lord with every fiber of our being.

The Pharisees had hoped to trick Jesus into saying that one part of the law was more important than another. However, Jesus knew the law. Instead of elevating one commandment above the others, the Lord summarized the entire law with a single command.

If you continue reading the book of Matthew, you'll see how quickly the Lord shut down all of his naysayers.

No one could trick Jesus; no one could refute Him. He is above all.

Seventeenth-century commentator Matthew Henry said of these verses:

An interpreter of the law asked our Lord a question, to try, not so much his knowledge, as his judgment. The love of God is the first and great commandment, and the sum of all the commands of the first table. Our love of God must be sincere, not in word and tongue only. All our love is too little to bestow upon him, therefore all the powers of the soul must be engaged for him, and carried out toward him.

Henry's words ring so true. We must love the Lord with our whole being.

We won't be able to give the Lord the adoration he deserves with only one part of us; we bring Him glory and praise by worshipping Him with everything we have and are.

As Henry said, "All the powers of the soul must be engaged for him."

Advent Prayer

Lord, thank You for the reminders, even in our food, of how wonderful You are and how much You take care of us. Thank You that today we can praise You with our hearts and our souls and our minds. Please continue to reveal to us ways we can serve You with our entire being.

Advent Activity

In your Kitchen, create a sweet and savory snack board with meaningful components for the heart, soul, and mind.

EXAMPLES

Food for the Heart:
- Dark Chocolate
- Walnuts
- Almonds
- Blueberries

Food for the Soul (AKA: food that makes you happy):
- Cheese
- Dates
- Cashews
- Peanut Butter
- Dark Chocolate

Food for the Mind:
- Blueberries
- Walnuts
- Almonds
- Avocado
- Dark Chocolate

You'll notice blueberries, dark chocolate, almonds, and cashews are good options for all three lists.

Lay the food on your board in the order you want to talk about them.

Gather your family around and read Matthew 22:37–38.

These foods represent things that are good for our hearts, our souls, and our minds.

When we eat these foods, our whole body will benefit.

We will have energy to think, strength for our heart to pump blood through our body, and satisfaction for our soul when we taste something delicious.

In the same way that these foods benefit our body as a whole, so our adoration for the Lord must come from our entire being.

CELEBRATING ADVENT IN THE

Activity Space

DAY 16

ANTICIPATION
of Advent

A *little* baby was coming to save a big world. A *little* manger would hold the greatest Savior in the world. A *little* town would set the stage for the biggest event in all of history.

But you, O Bethlehem of Ephrathah, who are one of the little clans of Judah, from you shall come forth for me one who is to rule in Israel, whose origin is from of old, from ancient days.
— Micah 5:2

Micah uses the description of "little" to describe Bethlehem because Bethlehem was so small, it wasn't even listed when Joshua and Nehemiah recounted significant cities. Check out Joshua 15:21–63 and Nehemiah 11:1–36 to see the list.

Bethlehem. So small, not even a mention among the cities of Judah.

Judah was comprised of many cities, all a part of the kingdom held by David and his descendants. Bethlehem was David's hometown, but it doesn't merit a mention when the territory of Judah is documented.

We know children can often feel unseen, unheard, and unable to do many of the things they'd like to do. Sometimes I wonder if this makes them feel insignificant?

Children can often hear they are "too small" to do something; too small to use a knife, to ride that big-kid bike, to shave like daddy does, to swing on the big-kid swing, to go down the tall slide, to pick up their baby brother, to wear mommy's makeup, etc.

But we as adults often hear the same sentiment wrapped in different words:

"We are going with another candidate for this job. Thank you for applying."

"I need to end this relationship, but I promise you are not the problem."

"You don't qualify for this."

"You don't measure up to that."

And on it goes.

When was the last time you also felt less than, insignificant, or not good enough? I'm sure if Bethlehem could "feel" anything, it would have felt insignificant and passed over.

This discussion brings a whole new meaning to the song "O Little Town of Bethlehem," doesn't it? Well, with Micah's prophecy, all eyes turned toward that little town.

Sometimes the Lord does the biggest things in the smallest of places. The Lord can move mountains in your life from your prayer closet. The Lord can change someone's entire life by simply nudging their heart. The Lord can raise up leaders to change the world from the pages of His Word. He doesn't need much room or a massive stage.

Advent Activity

Have your family members or friends think of the smallest, but most important, item they own. They can also think of their favorite childhood toy. If you have children, have them go and get the smallest toy they own.

Have each family member explain or contemplate the significance their item has in their life.

Why is that *little* item so important?

Read Micah 5:2 as a family. Tell them the story of the baby Jesus being born in a tiny little town called Bethlehem.

There can be tremendous significance in small things.

Even though children may be little, and even though you may feel inadequate at certain moments within your life, the Lord has big plans for each of us.

His big plans all started that day, in that tiny manger, in that small town of Bethlehem.

Take some time to sing, or listen to, "O Little Town of Bethlehem."

Advent Prayer

Thank You, Lord, for bringing us Jesus. Thank You for making seemingly insignificant things matter a great deal in Your kingdom. Thank You for our lives and the lives of all of the children around the world. Thank You for the big plans You have, even for the tiniest of hands.

ARRIVAL
of Advent

Jesus was here! He didn't arrive with a legion of angels, descending from heaven on clouds of glory. He didn't show up with an earthquake that would shake the world awake. Jesus arrived with tiny coos and small fingers wrapped around His mother's pinky.

Jesus was here, and he came to the world as a baby.

*And she gave birth to her firstborn son and wrapped him
in bands of cloth, and laid him in a manger,
because there was no place for them in the inn.*
– Luke 2:7

Bible teacher J. Vernon McGee described this exact moment, saying,

It is wonderful to see a little baby come into the world, and your heart goes out to him; there is a sympathy that goes from you to him. That is the way God entered the world. He could have entered—as He will when He comes to earth the second time—in power and great glory. Instead, He came in the weakest way possible, as a baby. George Macdonald put it this way:

They all were looking for a King

To slay their foes and lift them high:

Thou cam'st, a little baby thing

That made a woman cry.

That is the way the Saviour came into the world. He did not lay aside His deity; He laid aside His glory.

Jesus laid aside His glory, not His deity.

Pope Benedict XVI emphasized the humility of Jesus by focusing on the manger. He said, "The manger is the place where animals find their food. But now, lying in the manger, is he who called himself the true bread come down from heaven, the true nourishment that we need in order to be fully ourselves. This is the food that gives us true life, eternal life. Thus the manger becomes a reference to the table of God, to which we are invited so as to receive the bread of God."

What a powerful thought! Our Lord could have come to the earth in so many ways. He could have put everyone on notice with trumpets blaring and skies ablaze, but instead, He chose to come in the meekest and simplest of ways.

His chosen birth plan was not one that stripped Him of His divinity. Rather, it showed people that He didn't need the pomp and circumstance to prove He was Lord. In fact, His lowly entrance into our world pointed to His identity as the Bread of Life. He is the Savior whose body would be broken to give us new life.

How often have we wanted a stage or a grand moment for people to see us as something special?

Have you ever seen a little girl twirl around in a pretty dress, hoping those closest will take notice of her beauty?

Have you ever seen a little boy flex his muscles in a crowded room so he can be seen for the strength he bears?

When was the last time you longed to be noticed, seen, or heard for the wonder you are?

Just as God used tiny Bethlehem as the stage for the greatest show in the history of our world, He used a tiny little baby's cry of arrival to set in motion the greatest rescue in the world.

How often do we long for the grand praise of others? How often do we hope for recognition and public adoration?

Jesus's entrance into this world is proof we do not need the approval of man or the grandeur of this earth to solidify our status as His beloved. We just need to be reminded that we are sons and daughters of the one true King.

This world's accolades do not matter when compared to what our Lord thinks of us and how He sees us.

Advent Prayer

Jesus, thank You for coming to earth to save us. Thank You for showing us we do not need the grandest gestures and the biggest stages in order to find true meaning in this world. We already matter a great deal to God's kingdom, and You came so that we may have abundant life with You forever.

Advent Activity

You may remember a time as a child when you received a trophy, ribbon, or medal for a job well done in athletics or academics.

As children, we can look at these symbols as the measures of our worth, but no award can compare to knowing our worth in the eyes of God.

To help you remember this tiny King who came to give you life in God's kingdom, make a little crown to sit somewhere in your home this Advent season.

If you have children, this is a fun craft to do with them. Make the crown out of paper and tape or glue. It could also be fun to shop for something to represent this symbol in your home.

Every time you see that small token, you can utter a prayer of thanksgiving for the quiet way Jesus entered our world, as well as a prayer of hope that more people would come to know Him.

DAY 18

AWAKEN
to Advent

We must understand Jesus's humanity to truly understand Him.

He came to earth as a baby who would grow up and experience many of the same things we have experienced in life, yet He was fully divine as well.

Fully man, fully God.

He knew what it felt like to scrape your knee as a child. He knew what it was like to have your feelings wounded by someone's hurtful words. He knew what it was like to long for a dream yet unfulfilled. He knew what it was like to grieve a loved one's passing. He knew what it meant to be human.

Our connection to Him is realized through our understanding of His humanity. But, in order to fully awaken to who Jesus is, we must know His humanity while also acknowledging His deity.

And the Word became flesh and lived among us, and we have seen his glory, the glory as of a father's only son, full of grace and truth.
– John 1:14

The words "lived among us" here can also be translated "dwell." As we have referenced before in this devotional, *dwell* is a prominent word in the celebration of Advent. We've seen how the Lord longed to come and dwell among us, to take up residence with us.

"Dwell" is sometimes seen in other translations as He "pitched His tent." In Jesus's time, the people who lived in tents were often shepherds, sojourners, and soldiers. The reference to Jesus pitching a tent among us is referring to his position as all of those things in our lives—a shepherd, sojourner, and soldier—and when John uses "lived among us," that can also be translated to "pitched His tent among us."

Jesus's time on earth would be temporary and thus the comparison to a sojourner pointed to His purpose on this earth: to leave earth as a sacrifice for our sins.

There is a moment of awakening that comes when we recognize Jesus came for us and to be with us. He came to give us life eternal with Him and the Father, if we choose to invite Him into our hearts and homes as our Lord.

God longs to dwell in your heart, and in the spirit of this Advent season, He longs for His spirit of peace to dwell in your home.

Advent Activity

To demonstrate Jesus coming to earth and becoming the Word made flesh, we can use the activity of pitching a tent to reflect on Jesus's coming to dwell with us.

It may seem silly to do this if you are an adult, but if you have children around, this will be a fun activity.

Create some sort of "tent" in your home today.

For children, that can be a fort made of chairs and blankets, or for the adults, it could be a quiet moment outside under the stars or under the covers of your bed.

Wherever that space is, create it, and in that space read John 1:14.

Ponder the ways the Lord has "pitched a tent" in your heart and home.

Also think about the ways in which you long for Him to permeate your life and the lives of those around you this Christmas season.

Advent Prayer

Lord, thank You for sending Jesus to earth. Please continue to awaken within us a desire for His glory and His peace this Advent season. Please fill our home and the homes of those we love with Your presence, and bring those around us, who do not yet know You, to a saving knowledge of Your Son this season. May our hearts and our home be a "tent" where He dwells so that others may know Your presence.

DAY 19

ANOINTING
of Advent

J esus came to earth as Mediator between us and God
  the Father. Humanity dreamed of all kinds of saviors—
financial, political, and religious—but when God sent his Son to
earth, He anointed him in a way that human beings could hardly
imagine, much less possess. Once they experienced it, though,
they would long to be near it.

Jesus said to him, "I am the way, and the truth, and the life.
No one comes to the Father except through me."
– John 14:6

Jesus spoke these words almost thirty-three years after His birth, in conversation with His disciples not long before He would die on the cross. These followers had been with Him for years, watched His actions, listened to Him speak and proclaim good news, and yet they still struggled to fully understand His life and purpose.

This particular verse is Jesus's response to a question from Thomas. He wanted to know where Jesus was going, because Jesus had just announced He was going to prepare a place for His friends (verses 3–4).

Thomas was seeking a destination. He wanted a map, so he could find his way to the place the Lord was headed. Thomas was asking Jesus WHERE to go.

Jesus's response, "I am the way," told Thomas, and us today, that Jesus wouldn't be found in a physical destination, or by traveling to a certain place. The reason God sent His Son to earth to dwell among us was so we could be saved through a relationship with the Anointed One.

If the WAY to salvation is through a relationship with Jesus, then we must trust Him as the TRUTH, the fulfillment of all those prophecies that even Doubting Thomas would have seen.

And if the WAY to salvation is through a relationship with Jesus, and we trust Him as the TRUTH because of all He has done, then He is the only WAY to having TRUE LIFE.

Jesus Anointed is our path to God's throne, and the destination is eternal life with Him.

Advent Activity

If you have any maps in your home, take them out (or print some maps of your favorite places).

Look at the intricacies of the roads and think about how Thomas believed he needed a physical map to reach the Lord. How confusing that must have been for him!

If you have children, you can find toy cars and let them drive on the maps and pretend they are going to their favorite destinations.

As you look at the map, ask yourself or pose to the group these questions:

1. Have you ever felt the Lord was far away?
2. In your own life, how has the Lord been the way, the truth, and the life?
3. Do you need Jesus to come and show up in your life right now and be the way, the truth, and the life?

Once you are done with the maps, write the words WAY, TRUTH, and LIFE across one of them as a reminder of your journey to Jesus.

Advent Prayer

Lord, thank You that we do not have to drive a confusing road to find You. We do not even have to say a certain prayer to reach You. You are already here among us, in this room right now. You are here, and you came to give us life. You are the way to that life. Please make Yourself so real to us today.

ADORATION
of Advent

Our adoration for the Lord doesn't only come through in our words. It also comes through in our actions. You can tell someone all day long that you love them, but if you never show them love with your actions, they will never believe your words.

One of the best examples in Scripture of a person showing her adoration for the Lord comes from Mary of Bethany.

Mary took a pound of costly perfume made of pure nard,
anointed Jesus' feet, and wiped them with her hair.
The house was filled with the fragrance of the perfume.
— John 12:3

There's a lot to unpack here, and it's helpful to know some of the customs of the time to understand why this scene is so strange.

It was customary to wash a guest's feet when they entered your home, but it wasn't customary to wash their feet during dinner. Women didn't normally let their hair down, as Mary did, because it could be seen as a sign that the woman had loose morals. And finally, the perfume Mary used was very expensive— not the sort of thing used to wash the feet of a guest. The bottle would have been so costly and precious, it would have been saved for a long time, perhaps passed down to the next generation.

The entire Advent season reminds us of giving. We think of the Lord giving us Jesus. We think of Jesus giving us the gift of salvation. We think of giving gifts to one another. Giving is at the center of it all.

When you think about giving gifts to your loved ones, do you not want to give them the best gifts you can possibly afford?

If your children ask for certain gifts, even if they are opulent, do you not long to give them what they ask for?

Mary was demonstrating to the room, and ultimately to all of mankind, that love for the Lord is expressed by giving Him the best of what you have, your most prized gifts.

❦ Advent Prayer ❦

Jesus, thank You for the special people and possessions in our lives.
It is because of You that we have all of these wonderful blessings.
Please help us see opportunities to show our adoration to You and to
show others the love You have for them. May we always bring our
best selves to You, in worship and in praise.

Advent Activity

If you have children, ask them to go find the most important thing that they have and bring it to you.

If there are only adults around, ask them to get their most prized possession or think about what that might be. This exercise is most effective if you can be looking at the object you hold most dear.

Ask these questions:

1. Why is this item most important to you?
2. What kind of special care do you take of this item?
3. Does it have a special place where it resides to keep it safe or to serve as a reminder of its importance?

Before you read John 12:3 to your family, give some context for Mary and her decisions. Then read the verse to everyone.

Ask your family, "If Jesus needed this very special item you have, would you give it to Him?"

When we love, we give our very best. Mary's very best to offer Jesus, as an act of adoration to Him, was the most expensive thing she owned, this special perfume.

CELEBRATING ADVENT IN THE

Christmas Space

ANTICIPATION
of Advent

$\mathcal{M}$ost people notice it. Most people feel it. Most people anticipate it with bated breath, waiting for it all year long.

Commercials on television spin around your home with the sound of Coke fizzing and Santa laughing.

It makes your heart leap a bit, while also making you surprisingly thirsty.

Bells ring outside of stores as you shop. The sound resurrects memories you long to recreate over and over again. Christmas is now upon us—the season we've waited for all year long.

In many homes, this season is welcomed with decorations. Garlands, banners, wreaths, trees, ornaments, presents, stars, lights—you name it. Homes are filled with Christmas.

How do we invite our Lord into this space of commercial creativity? Where does He fit?

The verses below from Luke describe Mary, the mother of Jesus, visiting her cousin Elizabeth's home, right after Mary found out she was with child.

In those days Mary set out and went with haste to a Judean town in the hill country, where she entered the house of Zechariah and greeted Elizabeth. When Elizabeth heard Mary's greeting, the child leaped in her womb. And Elizabeth was filled with the Holy Spirit and exclaimed with a loud cry, "Blessed are you among women, and blessed is the fruit of your womb. And why has this happened to me, that the mother of my Lord comes to me? For as soon as I heard the sound of your greeting, the child in my womb leaped for joy. And blessed is she who believed that there would be a fulfillment of what was spoken to her by the Lord."

– Luke 1:39–45

Think of the joy Mary and Elizabeth both felt upon seeing one another and realizing they both were pregnant. These verses show the joy between two believers and how, when we come together, we can share the joys of the kingdom. The joy Mary felt filled Elizabeth's home with anticipation for the coming of the Messiah.

For I am longing to see you so that I may share with you some spiritual gift to strengthen you—or rather so that we may be mutually encouraged by each other's faith, both yours and mine.
– Romans 1:11-12

Mutually encouraged. Sharing gifts.

One of the greatest things about the Advent season is the sharing that takes place around the spaces we decorate for Christmas; and thus, how Jesus can permeate every area of our homes.

Set aside a guarded time to share encouragement with your family today.

Advent Activity

Gather in the light of your Christmas tree and practice one (or both) of these things:

1. Have each family member share something wonderful they are thanking the Lord for in this season. This is a way of encouraging one another in our faith.

2. Gather your family together and pass out cards (or paper) and pens. Ask that each person think of someone they want to write an encouraging note to this Advent season. It was nice for Mary and Elizabeth to be able to see one another and encourage each other. Practice encouragement with cards under the tree or mail you can send to loved ones you may not see.

Explain to your family the importance of having one another during this season.

Read Luke 1:39-45 and talk about what it means that Elizabeth's baby leapt in her womb.

What do you think the atmosphere in the room was like that day when all of this occurred?

How can you and your loved ones create the same atmosphere of mutual encouragement in your own home this season?

Advent Prayer

Thank you, Lord, for togetherness during this Advent season. Thank You for all of the ways we have counted Your goodness in our discussion tonight. Please be with our family and friends whom we will not see this season. Wrap them with Your love so they feel the joy of this season in their hearts and know the true reason we celebrate.

DAY 22

ARRIVAL
of Advent

Jesus has arrived. He is here. We no longer have to look to the future as the promised time, because it's happening now. The Christmas season is here. We no longer have to anticipate its arrival. It's upon us.

It is amazing how surely and confidently Isaiah stated his prophecies. He wrote long before Jesus's birth transpired, yet he spoke with so much certainty about the Messiah's coming that he often used the past tense, as if these things had already happened.

For a child has been born for us, a son given to us; authority rests upon his shoulders; and he is named Wonderful Counselor, Mighty God, Everlasting Father, Prince of Peace.
– Isaiah 9:6

We looked at this verse once already on Day 7, but this little verse in the Old Testament is packed with wisdom to unfold.

The Lord was teaching His people a lot about the Messiah in this one verse. Isaiah was telling us that the Messiah would be all we ever needed and much more than we could have ever wanted.

Jesus was not just a gift, He was THE GIFT.

As we wait for Christmas Day to arrive, people both young and old are longing to see wrapped gifts with their names on the tags.

What is in that box? Who is giving me the gift in that bag? Will I like what I have been given this year? Will they like what I have chosen for them?

We pick boxes and bags, ribbons and bows, wrapping paper and tissue paper, to wrap all of the gifts we have purchased for one another.

We take time to prepare the gift.

We cut the paper just right.

We tie the bow and fix it perfectly on top.

We long to make our sweet purchases look so pleasant and inviting under our trees.

The Lord was doing the same thing with the coming of Jesus.

The anticipation of Jesus being born was like seeing a box under the tree wrapped so neatly, adorned with the shiniest of bows.

Jesus's birth, as Isaiah foretold, was the unwrapping of the gift.

And what was inside?

A Wonderful Counselor.

A Mighty God.

An Everlasting Father.

A Prince of Peace.

Each of these names given to Jesus holds so much weight. We previously saw, when we celebrated Advent in the Dining Room, what it meant for Jesus to be Everlasting Father and the Prince of Peace.

Today, as we look at the first two titles in Isaiah's list, Wonderful Counselor and Mighty God, think about the space in your home where all of your gift giving, and maybe even some of the gift preparation, happens.

WONDERFUL COUNSELOR

The Hebrew word translated "wonderful" is related to a word used to describe God's mighty works and miracles.

The name "Wonderful," then, is describing the incredible gifts of deliverance and redemption that Jesus would bring to the world.

The people of Isaiah's time were looking for miracles; looking for a Savior who would come and take all of their problems away and leave them with "wonderful" lives. Could they really fathom what "wonderful" would mean? Could they understand that this Savior would be beyond what they could even imagine?

Our Wonderful Counselor knew what we needed in His perfect wisdom.

He is the source of your life in Christ Jesus,
who became for us wisdom from God,
– 1 Corinthians 1:30

If His wisdom is from God, then we know He is the ultimate Counselor to have in our lives.

How often have you needed sound advice from someone to help you make a decision? How often have you needed an ear to listen and help you sort out your thoughts?

Isaiah knew the Wonderful Counselor was coming to impart wisdom on all of His people and to all the world.

Jesus is the Savior who would give us wisdom from God and leave us speechless with the marvelous works He would perform.

What a miraculous gift of wisdom and knowledge!

MIGHTY GOD

The Hebrew word translated "mighty" is the word for "warrior."

Joshua 1:14 uses the same word when he says, "But all the warriors among you shall cross over armed before your kindred and shall help them" (emphasis added).

Isaiah was prophesying that Jesus would be the ultimate Warrior. He would fight on our behalf.

How often have we felt weary in the middle of life's battles? How often have we felt tired and in need of help? Isaiah was saying to us all, "Help is on the way."

Jesus was a gift, given us to be our mighty Savior, victorious in every battle. What an incredible gift of security.

Think about your life and where you are right now. Where are the places you need the help of a Wonderful Counselor? Where are the places you are longing for a Mighty God?

Jesus is here. He has arrived. He is ready and waiting to give you wisdom, and He fights for and protects His people.

Take some time to think about who you need Jesus to be this year.

DWELL

Advent Prayer

Lord, thank You for the gift You gave us by sending your Son to earth. You sent us a Savior who would be all the things we ever needed in a Messiah. Thank You for such a miraculous present! Help us to remember He is near when we need Him. Help us to remember Jesus is our Wonderful Counselor when we need wisdom, and help us to remember Jesus is our Mighty God, who goes to battle for us. Thank You, Lord, for all you are to us at every moment.

Advent Activity

Find some paper. By yourself, or together as a family, write down a prayer to the Lord. Share your longings for this season with Him, as well as what you are thankful for.

Write a prayer to the Lord asking Him to be your Counselor or thanking Him for the wisdom you have received from Him this past year.

Write a prayer to the Lord asking him to be Mighty God in a certain circumstance in your life or thanking Him for protecting you during a particular season or event this past year.

Have some gift-wrapping supplies ready, and have everyone wrap up their piece of paper with their prayer on it. Place your wrapped prayers under the tree with Jesus's name attached.

How great is it that as you offer the prayers of your heart, Jesus has already received them! You do not have to wait for Him to open the gift. He knows your desires before you speak them.

Be encouraged: He knows your heart, and He hears your prayers.

AWAKEN
to Advent

The wise men mentioned in Matthew's gospel were on a quest. They had seen a star rise in the night sky, and they set off in search of a newborn king.

When the star led them to the land of Israel, they went to Jerusalem, because that's where the people of those times would expect to find a king. They visited King Herod and shared that a new king had been born. Herod immediately feels threatened by this news. He asks the wise men to find this child who has been born king and report back to him.

⁂

When they had heard the king, they set out; and there, ahead of them, went the star that they had seen at its rising, until it stopped over the place where the child was. When they saw that the star had stopped, they were overwhelmed with joy. On entering the house, they saw the child with Mary his mother; and they knelt down and paid him homage. Then, opening their treasure chests, they offered him gifts of gold, frankincense, and myrrh.

– Matthew 2:9-11

This was the wise men's awakening moment. When they arrived and saw Jesus, they knelt down.

Their hearts had been telling them Jesus was special—that He was a king to be sought out—but upon seeing Him, they knew He was more than just a king; their posture said it all.

When you visit a young child, you don't kneel in his or her presence. The kneeling of the wise men was a posture of worship; it shows their immediate recognition of Jesus's deity.

People have assumed there were three wise men because of the three gifts—gold, frankincense, and myrrh—but Matthew doesn't actually tell us how many wise men there were. The gifts, however, may indicate more about Jesus than they do about the wise men who gave them.

The gold may have been a nod to Jesus's status as a king; the frankincense may allude to Jesus's divinity; and the myrrh may point to Jesus's death, since myrrh was often used as a fragrance in burials (see John 19:39).

One of the most telling moments of the wise men's awakening comes in Matthew 2:12: "And having been warned in a dream not to return to Herod, they left for their own country by another road."

The wise men had seen Jesus and knew he was the Messiah. They were not going back to tell Herod where to find this young boy that Herod wanted to destroy.

What wonderful visitors for Jesus to have early in His life.

Advent Activity

While some people use an angel, many people place a star at the top of their Christmas tree, a symbol of the story of the wise men in Matthew's gospel.

While we do not look to the shininess of that object to light our way to Jesus as the wise men did, we do see it hover above the gifts we place under our tree; in the same way the star hovered over the gift of Jesus.

The gifts under our trees are carefully chosen, having been picked with a meticulous eye for our family and friends. We selected items with meaning or ones that might fulfill longings our loved ones have. Just as the wise men brought Jesus gifts of meaning, so do we select gifts of purpose for those we love most.

Gather your loved ones around your Christmas tree and read Matthew 2:9–11.

Explain the story of the wise men and how, once they were awakened to who He was, they praised Him with gifts filled with meaning and with their protection and loyalty.

Have everyone look at the star on top of the tree and reflect on the story of the wise men.

Advent Prayer

Lord, thank You for the star You gave to light the way to Jesus. Thank You for showing the wise men just who Jesus was and for pricking their hearts to protect Him. Thank You for this time to reflect as a family in this space we use to celebrate Christmas every year. Thank You for the means to get one another gifts to love on each other during this season. May our gifts bring special meaning to those who receive them.

DAY 24

ANOINTING
of Advent

We've returned to Isaiah a number of times already in this devotional, as he prophesied in great detail Jesus's birth and life. We live on the other side of those prophecies now. Jesus has arrived.

The spirit of the Lord God is upon me, because the Lord has anointed me; he has sent me to bring good news to the oppressed, to bind up the brokenhearted, to proclaim liberty to the captives, and release to the prisoners; to proclaim the year of the Lord's favor, and the day of vengeance of our God; to comfort all who mourn.
— Isaiah 61:1-2

Isaiah was showing us that when the Messiah (Jesus) comes to earth, He would be anointed by God and do amazing works. He would bring good news, heal broken hearts, set people free, and comfort those in need. Who wouldn't want a Savior like that? He sounds amazing!

One of the most beautiful things about the Bible is seeing prophecy in the Old Testament fulfilled in the New Testament. In Luke, we see Jesus in the synagogue of Nazareth, His hometown.

When he came to Nazareth, where he had been brought up,
he went to the synagogue on the sabbath day, as was his custom. He
stood up to read, and the scroll of the prophet Isaiah was given to
him. He unrolled the scroll and found the place
where it was written: "The Spirit of the Lord is upon me,
because he has anointed me to bring good news to the poor.
He has sent me to proclaim release to the captives and recovery
of sight to the blind, to let the oppressed go free, to proclaim the year
of the Lord's favor." And he rolled up the scroll, gave it back
to the attendant, and sat down. The eyes of all in the synagogue
were fixed on him. Then he began to say to them,
"Today this scripture has been fulfilled in your hearing."
– Luke 4:16–21

You can almost sense a "mic drop" moment right here in the Bible. Jesus picks up a scroll that many people would have read to educate themselves about the coming Messiah, but this wasn't education for Jesus. He tells the people listening He's the one Isaiah was talking about.

This could give you chills just imagining what it would've been like, sitting in the synagogue as this was happening. The tension in the room must have been palpable.

The wonders Jesus performed were confirmation that He was the Messiah Isaiah had spoken of. Jesus was anointed to deliver on God's promises.

Look at God's promises concerning Jesus in Isaiah 61:1–2:

He would bring good news to the poor.

He would proclaim liberty to the captives.

He would proclaim release to the prisoners.

He would proclaim recovery of sight to the blind.

He would proclaim the year of the Lord's favor.

How could He plan to do all of this?

Because Jesus would deal with the root problem for all of humanity: sin.

Jesus's arrival has given all of us the opportunity to be free of our sin, if we will give our lives to Him.

No one is poor who has Jesus, because Jesus is worth more than the greatest treasure. No one is a prisoner who has Jesus, because He sets us free to love God and love others. No one is blind who has Jesus, because He gives us eyes to see the world as it truly is.

The gift of Christmas is more than we deserve, because of all the things that Jesus has come to be for us.

He is here.

He is here now.

And with Him is an anointing of freedom, sight, and eternal wealth for each and every one of us.

Advent Prayer

Jesus, thank You for coming to earth and for fulfilling the promises of God in our lives. Thank You for doing this so many years ago when You were on earth, but thank You for continuing to do this today in each of our lives. Our lives are so much richer, freer, and fuller because of You and Your love.

Advent Activity

Some families have the tradition of sending Christmas cards or writing a family newsletter this time of the year. They put photos in their cards or in their newsletter and give an update on everything their family has done during the past year.

This year, take the good news of Jesus and write letters of thanksgiving to the Lord for everything He's done for you this year.

You can keep the letters for yourself, place them under the tree as a gift, or mail copies to family and friends. Use the promises Jesus came to fulfill as the outline of your letter.

What has the Lord done for you this year that has made you realize just how truly rich you are?

What has the Lord done this year to make you realize the freedom you have in Him?

What has the Lord shown you this year that you may have been blind to in the past?

What favor has the Lord shown you this year?

DAY 25

ADORATION
of Advent

The wise men brought gifts to Jesus, but there was nothing He needed.

This is a fascinating aspect of the story of Jesus's birth: the realization that Jesus didn't really need what they were bringing. It's not just because gold, frankincense, and myrrh don't make great toddler toys, or because Jesus as a toddler wasn't able to actually do anything with those gifts. Instead, the irony, and maybe a bit of sacred comedy, is that Jesus at the moment of that visit was presiding over all of creation.

Jesus already had the whole world.

Ascribe to the Lord the glory due his name; bring an offering, and come before him. Worship the Lord in holy splendor.
– 1 Chronicles 16:29

The writer of 1 Chronicles, who may have been Ezra, is quoting a psalm of David here: "Ascribe to the Lord the glory of his name; worship the Lord in holy splendor" (Psalm 29:2).

When the writer says "ascribe to the Lord," he's saying, give God what is already supposed to be His: glory and adoration.

Tremble before him, all the earth. The world is firmly established; it shall never be moved. Let the heavens be glad, and let the earth rejoice, and let them say among the nations, The Lord is king! Let the sea roar, and all that fills it; let the field exult, and everything in it. Then shall the trees of the forest sing for joy before the Lord, for he comes to judge the earth. O give thanks to the Lord, for he is good; for his steadfast love endures forever.

– 1 Chronicles 16:30-34

The Bible tells us time and time again that if we, the people of God, do not give adoration to the Lord, or do not know how to, the earth does. If you find yourself wondering how to show proper adoration to the Lord this season, look to His creation. As 1 Chronicles continues, the sea roars to glorify God and the trees sing to honor Him. If you look to creation today, you might find a bright white blanket of snow, or the fresh scent of a cedar tree, or a reverent stillness outside.

As we approach the Lord today, on the day we celebrate His birth, may we approach Him in worship, giving Him the glory He deserves, just as the heavens and earth declare His glory.

Jesus has filled your home this season in every way possible. As you've reflected on the season of Advent in the spaces of your home, you now celebrate—He dwells among and within us. In

Advent Activity

Many of us decorate our homes on the inside and on the outside at Christmastime. You may have lights strung up or a single wreath on the front door. However you and your family decorate the exterior of your home for Christmas, gather your loved ones outside today for a time of reflection.

Read aloud 1 Chronicles 16:29–34.

Instruct everyone to find the trees, look at the sky, notice the snow or the grass, then tell them to close their eyes and feel the air on their faces.

All of creation rises up to declare God's glory. Each sway of air, each rustle of a tree, each flurry of snow, and each wisp of a cloud call out the glory of God. When sweet baby Jesus's first little cry and coo exclaimed from His mouth, He was also adoring His Father in heaven as the Maker and Creator of all things.

Let us do the same with our prayerful adoration of Jesus this season.

doing so, Jesus's birth is our eternal gift. If there were ever a day to give Him the glory due His name, today is the day.

Advent Prayer

Jesus, thank You for the gift of creation and how it continually declares Your glory. Show us how to live lives that offer worship and praise to Your name this Advent season. May our homes be filled with adoration for You not only this season, but all year long.

Notes

LIVING ROOM:

Day 2: Matthew Henry, *A Commentary Upon the Holy Bible: Volume 5* (London: Religious Tract Society, 1835), 5.

Day 3: C. H. Spurgeon, *Devotional Classics of C. H. Spurgeon* (Lafayette, IN: Sovereign Grace Publishers, 2008), 332.

Day 4: Andrew Murray, *The Holiest of All, An Exposition of the Epistle to the Hebrews* (London: James Nisbet, 1895), 57.

Day 5: C. H. Spurgeon, "Acceptable Service," (sermon, London, January 15, 1882), Christian Classics Ethereal Library, https://www.ccel.org/ccel/spurgeon/sermons28.iii.html.

DINING ROOM:

Day 7: Brennan Manning, *The Relentless Tenderness of Jesus* (Grand Rapids, MI: Baker Book House, 2004), 208.

Day 7: "Isaiah 9 Commentary," Precept Austin, last modified December 12, 2018, https://www.preceptaustin.org/isaiah_9_commentary#9:6.

Day 8: Sir William Robertson Nicoll, ed., *The Expositor's Greek Testament, Volume 1* (New York: Dodd, Mead, 1897), 68.

NOTES

KITCHEN:

Day 13: Suzanne Tilton, *Through the Year with Martin Luther: A Selection of Sermons Celebrating the Feasts and Seasons of the Christian Year* (Peabody, MA: Hendrickson Publishers, 2007), 104.

Day 13: Arabah Joy, "How to Share the Gospel Using a Candy Cane," *Arabah Joy* (blog), December 2, 2015, https://arabahjoy.com/share-the-gospel-using-candy-cane/.

Day 15: Matthew Henry, *Matthew Henry's Concise Commentary on the Bible* (Grand Rapids, MI: Christian Classics Ethereal Library, 2011), 699.

ACTIVITY SPACE

Day 17: J. Vernon McGee, *Thru the Bible Vol. 37: The Gospels (Luke)* (Nashville: Thomas Nelson, 1995), chap. 2, EPUB.

Day 17: Joseph Ratzinger (Pope Benedict XVI), *Jesus of Nazareth: The Infancy Narratives* (New York: Crown Publishing Group, 2012), 68.

Day 20: David Guzik, "John 12—The Hour Has Come," Enduring Word, 2018, accessed June 8, 2020, https://enduringword.com/bible-commentary/john-12/.

Photo Attribution

Front Cover - © Yuriy Kovtun / istockphoto.com

Back Cover - © createvil / shutterstock.com

Pg. 16 - © Farmuty / stock.adobe.com

Pg. 18 - © Flaffy / shutterstock.com

Pg. 28 - © Konstantin Malkov / 123rf.com

Pg. 30 - © Vladeep / shutterstock.com

Pg. 32 - © barol16 / istockphoto.com

Pg. 33 - © aberheide / 123rf.com

Pg. 34 - © New Africa / stock.adobe.com

Pg. 35 - © Tabitazn / istockphoto.com

Pg. 36 - © New Africa / stock.adobe.com

Pg. 38 - © povareshka3 / 123rf.com

Pg. 40 - © maximleshkovich / 123rf.com

Pg. 42 - © povareshka3 / 123rf.com

Pg. 45 - © Oleksandra Pokhodzhay / 123rf.com

Pg. 50 - © kovaleva_ka / stock.adobe.com

Pg. 51 - © Olga Yastremska / 123rf.com

Pg. 52 - © serezniy / 123rf.com

Pg. 54 - © frizza / stock.adobe.com

Pg. 56 - © david_franklin / stock.adobe.com

Pg. 59 - © Anna Nahabed / 123rf.com

Pg. 61 - © Tabitazn iStock

Pg. 63 - © los_angela / istockphoto.com

Pg. 64 - © Pixel-Shot / stock.adobe.com

Pg. 66 - © Oksana Mironova / 123rf.com

Pg. 68 - © Ekaterina Senyutina / 123rf.com

Pg. 70 - © Santiaga / istockphoto.com

Pg. 72 - © povareshka3 / 123rf.com

Pg. 73 - © oksana_bondar / stock.adobe.com

Pg. 74 - © Lana U / shutterstock.com

Pg. 75 - © Ivan Zamurovic / 123rf.com

Pg. 78 - © ammentorp / 123rf.com

Pg. 81 - © Artem Kudryavtsev / 123rf.com

Pg. 82 - © Elena Veselova / 123rf.com

Pg. 84 - © sonyachny / stock.adobe.com

Pg. 86 - © Alla Rudenko / 123rf.com

Pg. 87 - © Oksana Bratanova / 123rf.com

Pg. 88 - © LukaTDB / istockphoto.com

PHOTO ATTRIBUTION

Pg. 91 - © Karavanska Alina / shutterstock.com

Pg. 92 - © David Cabrera Navarro / 123rf.com

Pg. 94 - © svetikd / istockphoto.com

Pg. 96 - © xxmmxx / istockphoto.com

Pg. 97 - © Anna Pustynnikova / 123rf.com

Pg. 98 - © Zakharov Zakharov / 123rf.com

Pg. 101 - © skynesher / istockphoto.com

Pg. 102 - © Yulia Mikhaylova / 123rf.com

Pg. 109 - © Tarik Kizilkaya / istockphoto.com

Pg. 110 - © Povareshka / istockphoto.com

Pg. 112 - © Switlana Symonenko / 123rf.com

Pg. 118 - © Jozef Polc / 123rf.com

Pg. 120 - © Olga Yastremska / 123rf.com

Pg. 121 - © Evgeny Atamanenko / 123rf.com

Pg. 122 - © balinature / 123rf.com

Pg. 123 - © Natalia Bodrova / 123rf.com

Pg. 124 - © MsDianaZ / shutterstock.com

Pg. 126 - © povareshka3 / 123rf.com

Pg. 127 - © Kirill Kedrinski / 123rf.com

Pg. 129 - © Iaroslav Danylchenko / 123rf.com

Pg. 130 - © Orbon Alija / istockphoto.com

Pg. 132 - © Oksana Mironova / 123rf.com

Pg. 136 - © Cathy Yeulet / 123rf.com

Pg. 138 - © Valentina Gabdrakipova / 123rf.com

Pg. 140 - © linghaa / stock.adobe.com

Pg. 141 - © happy_author / stock.adobe.com

Pg. 142 - © Nadezhda Gorodetskaya / 123rf.com

Pg. 144 - © Iulia Cozlenco / 123rf.com

Pg. 147 - © LiliGraphie / stock.adobe.com

Pg. 148 - © povareshka3 / 123rf.com

Pg. 149 - © elenabatkova / 123rf.com

Pg. 150 - © fotostorm / istockphoto.com

Pg. 154 - © GWImages / shutterstock.com

Pg. 155 - © JeanRee / istockphoto.com

Pg. 152 - @ Andrii Kucher / 123rf.com

Pg. 156 - © Switlana Symonenko / 123rf.com

Pg. 157 - © povareshka3 / 123rf.com

Pg. 159 - © lightfieldstudios / 123rf.com

Pg. 163 - © Oksana Mironova / 123rf.com

Pg. 166 - © kinderkz / stock.adobe.com

Pg. 167 - © povareshka3 / 123rf.com

Pg. 168 - © 2Mmedia / istockphoto.com

About Dexterity

Dexterity is an IBPA award-winning indie publisher based in Nashville, TN. We describe ourselves as "Book People with Startup Hustle," and our team, including the Dexterity Collective of fifty-plus book publishing professionals, believes in the power of books to make a difference. From editorial development to production, strategic consulting to data analytics, and from digital-only distribution to full-service sales representation, we not only publish our own titles—we make our menu of publishing services available to publishers and indie authors everywhere.